AF255235

Published in 2014

Copyright © by Trevor Martinson

No part of this book may be reproduced without written permission from the author

ISBN: 978-1-291-71948-2

Building Windmills

Trevor Martinson

"When the winds of change come, some will build walls whilst others will build windmills".

Chinese Proverb

Introduction

One day whilst walking through the wilderness, a man happened upon a vicious tiger. He ran but soon came to the edge of a cliff where the tiger stayed growling at the top. Climbing down a vine, he discovered another agitated tiger at the bottom who was growling and looking up at him and so he was stuck. Two rats then appeared and began gnawing on the vine he was holding. Whilst hanging there in this precarious position, the man noticed a plump red strawberry growing, so he reached for it and ate it, remarking to himself how delicious it was.

This Zen story tells us not to dwell on the past and don't worry about the future but to experience and cherish the moment of now and act accordingly to the situation that arises...............................This is a wonderfully simple story and I love it for the message it gives. My story here is from 2009 through to the end of 2012, and it is told through my poetry. I see this as a poetry book with added prose for context and to help you get inside my head - may God have mercy upon your soul if you manage such a thing!

I know the risk is that you the reader will focus on the narrative and breeze through the poems giving them a cursory read, but I implore you to resist this temptation. The poetry, whatever you think of it, is why I wrote the prose, not the other way round so please give it a chance! But be warned - Every storyteller will choose their story for a reason, and tell it in their way, perhaps changing the focus away from the main character, perhaps adding extra darkness and fear where there wasn't any before, perhaps taking myth and folklore and retelling it as truth. I will tell this story my way, and that will mean that my imperfections (for there are many) may be underplayed, and those of others are emphasised more. This subtle shift of emphasis is simply a reflection of how my mind has stored the events of my life, marriage, separation and all emotions beyond.

It may be a melodramatic statement to say that poetry has kept me sane, however, that I wrote poetry was certainly a big factor in me making it through these years. It became a process by which I cleared my mind, contextualised things and at the same time saving a fortune on therapy. To start from 2009 means there are 35 years of life including 11 years of marriage up to that point to condense into this introduction which makes condensing elaborate thoughts about the wonder of the universe into a Haiku seem easy. So I will use a couple of examples from that time to set the scene.

On the night in 1997 when I proposed, there was no excitement shown in her face, just the question back of "so why do you want to marry me?" This was on a Saturday evening and I must have passed the cross examination successfully as I got my positive reply 24 hours later, without fanfare it is true, but I got it. This was hardly an explosion of passion and joy, though of course in naive love untainted by hurt, this alarm was never going to penetrate through the reverberating wall of excitement, nerves and family noise. Jumping to our wedding day, I was the last to arrive at the registrar's office. I am never late for anything. I hate it. There is something in my DNA that abhors sloppy, 'I don't care' lateness. But on my wedding day I find myself delaying and procrastinating................. So I arrive at the registry office with my best man after the bride-to-be and all our families. I arrive to a potentially combustible mixture of relief and annoyance from all. I also arrive to see her with henna tattoos all over her hands. I know nothing about henna or the significance of its relationship with weddings and certainly didn't know that she was going to do this. Later that day, ever the romantic, she told me that she hadn't said anything about it because she thought I would try and talk her out of it and not understand. I

2

wouldn't have understood about henna if she had told me, as I didn't know about it, but talk her out of it? Looking back the signs were there. But, that was the 27th June 1998, I was 24 and she was 28.

Name changes played a significant part in our lives from the 1998 wedding to 2012 and may well be taken as a tangible insight into the minds of ungrounded people, of changing relationships, and a challenging of what marriage means all layered on top of historical extended families issues. In those 14 years, the person I married, now called Maria, has changed her Christian name once. She also gave herself a middle name, having been born without one, and then has since changed it twice more since that initial self-gift. She went from her maiden name to my boyhood name when married as is the norm although this was "much to my own surprise" which is a quote taken from her wedding speech. This was the name into which Zoe was born, and then we changed our surname, and this was the one into which Ed was born. Since then, she has changed her surname again to something completely different but which has extended family significance. I myself simply removed my middle name at the time of changing our surname and I think I am done with just the one change. I hope Maria is now happy with her current combination and it helps her be who she thinks she is or wants to be, but time will tell. On the whole though, our families seemed to cope exceptionally well, or at least they never let on much to us.

The birth of Zoe in 2003 and Ed in 2006 were indeed the much heralded 'life changing experiences' that are so often spoken about but so little understood until they are lived through. The experience of nearly losing Zoe as she was born should have brought us closer together, but didn't, and the strain on all of us after Ed was born was almost too much to bear. The decision to home educate was one made with our daughter's welfare at its heart, but it was also a lifestyle choice which Maria wanted and this juxtaposes my job as a manger within a big supermarket chain which loomed heavy over our marriage. Was I worrying too much? Was I working too many hours? Was I working for a 'big bad company?' Different people in my life have different views, and my opinion isn't one of fixed stubbornness. I can see the arguments of the extremes and I oscillate around the middle of the extreme views depending upon circumstance and mood. What I am certain of is that my move into Human Resources, and the three years of combining full time work with part time University studies with Zoe around and Ed being born during this time as well changed me forever as a human and made me stronger, but also pushed me out of the house and away from my family even more.

During this time in a different part of the country, Angela was unknown to me and living her own life, marrying just one week before I did in 1998…

So we start now in 2009;

Chapter 1

2009 begins to a backdrop of growing unrest, uneasiness, hard work, children, – Life in other words. The rather basic Haiku form poem I wrote in April 2009 and the poem of July 2009 paints a picture of where my mind was at this time. Although even having written these poems, I wasn't clear that I was stuck, lost, wanting more and should be fighting to get out – I just thought that this was life.

Haiku No 4 (April 2009)

deeply unhappy
Winter, Summer, Spring, Autumn,
deeply unhappy

My Prayer (July 2009)

So here I am God,
if you exist,
here I am waiting for you.
Reveal yourself Buddha,
for your enlightenment journey,
I am begging to begin.
Are you there Mohammad?
Coerce or cajole me,
force me to believe your way.
I am a beached whale,
a discharged disorientated soldier,
a drunken teenager,
another drifting soul of 2009.

So here I am God,
if you exist,
here I am waiting for you.
Is my time now?

Not enveloped youthfully,
not yet panicky, close to death,
just middle ground, average, bored.

Reveal yourself Buddha,
for your enlightenment journey,
I am begging to begin.
Jealousy of the converted,
their purpose and belief,
the energy and conviction,
aware of their passion.

Are you there Mohammad?
Coerce or cajole me,
force me to believe your way.
Cease the questioning for meaning,
illustrate and illuminate,
brand your message,
across the top of my brain.

So here I am God,
if you exist,
here I am waiting for you.

In early 2009 I was beginning to be open to the idea of religion. Would I find what I needed through religion? In essence no. However, I did start to hide myself away in books, and I did read around Buddhism alongside escapism into classic literature. All of this was alongside writing poetry myself and was an aid to distract me, inspire me, help my mind expand and to start a journey of discovery to begin to understand me and equally as important to try and understand others.

As October 2009 comes around I know that Maria and I no longer fit together well. I know we are seriously starting to fall apart but in the traditional manner I basically try and ignore it. I know I feel inferior to the friends she eulogises about, and I know this has been building up to now have a massive impact on my mental wellbeing. Somewhere in this building turmoil, I decide to have a tattoo. Mid-life crisis? Rebellion? I don't believe so but I can see why people thought it. I prefer to think of it as the first tangible act of calling out to the world who I really am. For many years I was troubled by the recurring thought of wanting to do it, but never feeling quite able to take that step forward. The reason for the reticence was fear. Fear of making the wrong choice of tattoo, fear of the unknown pain, fear of what Maria would say or think, fear of stepping out and into the light I project onto the world. For reasons I have never yet been able to crystallise enough to express, I decide to go for a ying / yang symbol on my left arm.

It was right (October 2009)

From the burden of denial and fear,
the implicit knowledge gestated,
now consciously aware that it was simply the time.
No more hiding or forcing,
just internal calmness,
and absolute trust that it was right.
No permission sought or needed,
but surprise and doubt hurled out like stones as a test,
but doubt, have faith, was not forthcoming.
But
now
the
heart is
pumping,
music blaring,
the first
ink marking
touch and,
"is that all?"
The relief,
Excitement!
But,
a body,
under,
attack,
reacts,
internalises,
shuts down,
defends
itself.
Slows down thought and movement,
until the artwork is complete,
the achievement upon completion introspective.
No more hiding or forcing,
just internal calmness,
and absolute trust that it was right.

I imagine myself reading the middle section in an urban, street, youth style rap.................. not exactly me, but I like to imagine. The reference to my body reacting was that whilst I didn't feel any pain whilst having it done, about 3 minutes in from the start I became incredibly hot, dizzy and then promptly passed out. What a man I am. I quickly came round highly embarrassed, but the artist took it all in his stride, although he said little. We waited around for 10 minutes for me to feel better and knock back some Coke before he carried on, with me still feeling embarrassed about it, part wanting to run out, but also knowing that there was no way that I was going to leave with it less than half finished. Ever the pragmatist. If I had left then, I would never have returned.

From around this time until Christmas 2009, life, relationships and all that I knew started to spiral out of control and started to become too big to contain inside my head. It started to hit home that actually something has been dying between us for too long to deny it any more – although to be fair I did stubbornly keep trying to do just that. Maria's infatuation with everything that I was not, and everything she felt she wanted became encapsulated and crystallised in a mutual 'friend'. History has since played this man to be totally innocent in the flirting, testing, and pushing of friendship boundaries – I'm not so sure, but ultimately it doesn't matter. When Maria got up from my side in bed to send him an email one day at 5am asking for confirmation of their relationship and the future, this freaked him out enough to declare his version of the truth to his partner, and the dam was broken. Friends made their choices, some trying to balance all of us, some blanking Maria and some completely unable to broach the subject with me. In a very bizarre way which I have never been able to satisfactorily explain, I was the one who stood by her most staunchly, I showed myself to be a true friend whilst others hid their head or retreated perhaps in fear that she may try and snare their partner next. Maria and I were forced to discuss their relationship, our relationship, everything I wasn't and most terrifying of all, the future. There were tears it is true, but it is also true to say that there were few raised voices and certainly no childish tantrums. Discussions were had about what to do, how we could move on, did we want to move on together, all enveloped by a million questions and fragments of exploding emotions that I could never quite grasp enough of to contextualise and articulate.

Chapter 2

January 2010 brought an unsteady peace. A declaration of 'trying to change' and to 'make things work'. A genuine, admirable attempt on both sides which gave rise to a moment of clarity and excitement in my mind which helped to produce the optimistic poem "Every Kiss"

Every Kiss (January 2010)

An antidote to living in a chloroform haze,
enlightenment achieved, nothing is forever,
a near terminal experience circumvented,
now every kiss really does have depth and meaning.

Out of the death of a thousand bad habits,
rises forth new pathways and cerebral connections,
the shared road of life needed a new junction created,
now every hand held is a tingling sensation.

With a life smashed like ice dropped onto frozen forest water,
the unexpected breath of a second chance came,
with less being more, brought less fear in conversation,
now every relaxed smile exchanged is a simple and real pleasure.

However within weeks of feeling and writing the poem, my statement above of 'nothing is forever' came, once again to mock me and prod me, safe in the knowledge I was unable to fight back. One Sunday morning as I was in the kitchen innocently reading the sports section of the Sunday Times, Maria casually announced that she no longer wanted to wear her wedding ring. The walk we took as a family in Romsey later that morning was not relaxed. That I was falling apart was in no way helped by Maria's complete normality within the situation. Unsurprisingly it was soon after this incident that the unsteady peace brokered before failed. Even at this point though, I wasn't angry. Sad, frustrated, in denial yes, but as her words told me that we had to do something different, that one of us had to move out and the reasons why, I was still not angry.

(Unsubtle author note - The bracketed second title is made up of the third word of each stanza's first line)

How Her Words Came - (Looking Towards Her But Not Knowing) - (Feb 2010)

They came looking for life not death,
they came looking for a resolution,
marching on a diet of frustration,
exhausted senses numbed to pain.

They came towards my lost soul,
they came towards mediocrity,
as judged by the magnificence,
of the idolised comparators.

They came, her voice the conduit,
they came, her words of change,
germinated because of blindness,
bedfellows of familiarity and malaise.

They came, but reserved at first,
they came, but now bounded by necessity,
an outpouring of feelings released,
mostly truth, some misreading, some things just plain wrong.

They came not with malice,
they came not out of hate,
but with exposed emotion,
antipathy to continue to fight.

They came knowing the risk,
they came knowing what may ensue,
arduous to reflect anger back,
since in advance all this she knew.

As my marriage officially imploded, I took time off work which in itself was a very rare occurrence. Only 4 days, but this was more than may have been expected by others. I took myself out of circulation for a while including time in Lymington to look at the boats and be calmed by the movement of the water and the normality of life happening around me. I also cycled in the forest to boost my energy levels and feel the beauty that the forest just infuses with you even in your lowest mood. At this point in my life, I was beginning to realise that writing poetry was therapy for me. It was sat near a river on an unusually warm day, during these 4 days off that 'Relax into Wealth' / 'But Still I Dare to Dream' came into my head and into my life to help start the long, slow process of healing wounds. Relax into Wealth is the name of a book that Maria was obsessed by. She would randomly turn to a page, read it and then contemplate its meaning on her life. I often felt it was this book that was driving the decision making process at this point. The key message as I heard it was that if people try and force things, this stops it from happening. But the approach seems to be to relax and be confident that when the time is right, what we need will be there for us. One should believe that the earth has an abundance of everything we need and that we will be ready for it when what we want will come to us. This was the starting point of the poem at this point in my life. I knew that with this mind set, if I tried to force my marriage back together, if I shouted, demanded, became a smothering romantic and trying too hard, this was simply doomed to fail. The alternative title was added by me a year or so later after sharing it at a local Poetry Society meeting where the 'Relax into Wealth' title was felt to be misleading. This was without the background knowledge of the book of course. So 'Relax into Wealth' is my title, and 'But Still I Dare to Dream' is for others.

**'Relax into Wealth' or 'But Still I Dare to Dream' -
(March 2010)**

Early spring,
and tall trees tower,
warm sunshine assimilates with me,
a woodpecker does as a woodpecker should.

I sit motionless, thinking, blinking, barely breathing,
aching for my wife's lost love to regenerate and reunite us,
knowing that should I chase it, seek it, force it,
that it will surely never come,
yet if I don't pursue,
then,
perhaps,
it might.

Should a mirage created as a love child of optimism and
despair materialise,
deny it access, stand firm and proud,
denounce the raising of hopes unilaterally,
as it is surely only in one persons mind; mine.

A gaze held momentarily too long,
accept it simply as shadows of the past,
make no attempt to grab for it,
move forward in small steps understanding the new content of
your heart.

Accepting the benefits of the swirling hurt of a thousand
regrets,
each tear releases droplets of pain,
keep memories of good and bad in tact,
but still I dare to dream.

Separating couples happen all the time. People giving birth happens all the time. People die all the time. This knowledge doesn't take away the immediacy and intimacy you face when it happens to you. I had allowed myself to be been bullied into feeling that I was not the 'right' person for Maria. Not just in the 3 months since December, but for years beforehand and probably the inferiority was planted when we first met and she introduced herself as an 'environmental scientist' and my first thought was simply "fucking hell"...............................I was an assistant department manager in a supermarket which is hardly comparable. The point was that I was beating myself up, continued to beat myself up and was never encouraged to feel equal to previous boyfriends, mutual friends or indeed anyone in our joint sphere of existence. At this moment in my life as my marriage was collapsing, *all* I could think about was us. The last few years were replaying over and over in my mind, the whole of my married life was replaying over and over, what I had done wrong, what I could do to make it right, over and over and over and over, all consuming, all powerful and totally dominant. Within a very short space of time I felt close to breaking point, not sure how to react, not caring about much. As a defence mechanism which my brain took it upon itself to give me, I became conscious of a silence, a black shadow, an absence of thought about Maria, about the failure, about worrying about the future, about the pain. This respite from the emotional turmoil whilst in itself was a moment of pure bliss, euphoria and peacefulness, suddenly gave way to a feeling of another negative emotion which simply lay on top of the ones that were just starting to settle - guilt.

Guilt of that Momentary Respite (March 2010)

I was entered unconsentually,
cerebrally raped,
I was cold and unaccepting,
in denial of my impending life steps.
Evolving and smothering waves of words,
non-stop free flowing emotions of loss,
becoming intrinsic to my every movement,
my every draw of breath.
The fitful sleep of a cold man infuses,
with the narcotic mimicking, turning, merging ,distorting lines
between reality and dreams,
conjoined with unrestrained memories and regrets.
As a child who craves dizziness,
my mind and resolve spinning out of control,
a shadow of pure blackness,
has arrived now at my side.
Only seconds consciously passed at first,
then minutes, slowed down minutes,
now forty minutes have dissolved through distraction,
the shadow's absence sidles into my consciousness.
The infant joy of peacefulness destroyed,
as the spectre of the returning shadow, seen,
bringing now another emotion,
guilt of that momentary respite.

Chapter 3

On the Monday I returned to work following my 4 days off, I held a very difficult meeting with my immediate team where I explained to them the situation as best I could, bearing in mind that I was not altogether sure of the facts myself. I explained that Maria and I had split up (not sure of the words I used, not really clear myself at that point), that we were all still in the house and that the kids were the main priority. After this, I went and cried in the toilets and tried to act as normal as I could at work which I impressively managed to do. Angela was in this meeting and she shudders when recalling it, both because of my emotions displayed, and hers kept hidden.

Following the traditional route, Maria and I decided that I should move out and I searched for flats and found one. We are behaving incredibly normally still at this stage. No hatred and little anger. I even got as far as putting the deposit down on a flat in the outskirts of Romsey on a wet, dark and windy Friday evening, rushing to the estate agents before it closed for the weekend. The overriding emotion I felt, or in reality didn't feel as I waited in the estate agents was numbness. This was mixed with some sadness, but mostly numbness. However, before I could move in, there was a hurried change of plan which saw Maria panic and feel the need to move out herself. She needed more space away from the house, me and the kids and as with so much in our marriage, she got what she wanted. That I wanted her to see the flat that I thought about moving into before I agreed to it was different to her approach. She told me that she had agreed a place after it was all completed. She didn't need me but I still needed and wanted her. I was off the pace once again.

Don't get me wrong, I know it was tough for her too (June 2010)

Our kids cried when she went to the flat,
the first night that she did.
But they fell asleep reassured
that she would return in the morning,
but the morning,
can take such a long time to come.
And me, waking at three
with my stomach seemingly
trying to come out through my eyes..........
............oh, and my clock hates me!
It ticks more loudly than last night
and its hands mock me by defying time
and moving so fucking slowly,
that they are trying to drive me insane.
So the clock hates me and I hate the clock.
And my heart is keeping time
with hummingbirds wings.
I feel emotion morph into tears
and I have sadness and regret enough
to keep me crying until the morning.
So, I also know that sometimes the morning,
sometimes the morning,
sometimes the morning
        can take such a long time to come.

So this became the norm for us, if slightly dysfunctional to the normal norm. Maria would spend the day at the house with the kids whilst I worked, and then go to the flat in the evening and come back to the house in the morning for me to go to work. Some nights she would stay at the house if it was more practical to do so. This separation from each other was seemingly what we both needed. We loosely agreed that we needed time, and we would see how things were working out between us at some point in the autumn. Although I was completely unaware of it at the time, Maria felt she could see that I was 'coming alive' again and was being forced to think for myself more, make decisions and not just wait for life to happen to me. Maria had the space she craved, and the kids and I even spent a night a couple of times with her at her place, treating it as a night away on holiday. It was tough for me though and I was never really relaxed in what was totally her domain. It did however open my eyes to see how different a living environment could be, rather than being bogged down by the walls and garden which we had lived in for over 10 years.

Maria and I became closer again and whilst this was wonderful, it did cause my brain to become further confused, twisted and entangled in itself. Any thoughts I had that the universe may conform to what I thought I needed, and what I desired were viciously snapped back from in front of me by the events one July evening.

A foreboding wisp (July 2010)

In harmonious song and symmetry,
flowing fauna regeneration,
and a new life channel being forged.
Circumstances fluid, new sediments of routines,
a fresh version of normality released,
as birdsong serenades me into Spring.

Premeditated abstinence of feelings agreed,
until Summer and Autumn are hence intertwined,
solace sought and comfort found by looking for strength
within.
An insatiable human ability for denial,
projecting control, rebuilding the self,
through the anticipated early Summer days yet to be played
out.

The tentative finding of friendship anew,
a relaxed evening, defences seconded out of sight,
two people together, not trying to be one.
Short term memories short circuited, circumvented,
a step into delusional deceit,
such a beautiful world within which to exist.

Yet suppressed emotions are uncontrollable,
the temporary taboo of deeply believed love,
articulated, released, rushed out on an impulse.
The emotional flash too wearying to wear,
take refuge, envelop under a pretty veil,
still grieving the loss, caring again, knowing I never stopped.

Out of control, fearful of passion,
rebuilding the self? Repugnance of self,
inadequacy again at the awkwardness caused.
The reminiscent wisp of feeling, futuristically cast,
bore fear, so scared of being hurt again,
by the same person in the same way.

My confidence, as so often before was once again knocked and the reality of the situation hit me full on. I had broken the 'Relax into Wealth' rules and I felt the retribution from my mistake hit me low and hard. After the ripping open of the partially healed wounds had caused cries of anguish, I could have reacted in a number of ways. My response, impressively I think, was to once again begin to adapt to my surroundings and this started to induce a weird sense of freedom and just the tiniest touch of excitement.

One example of this was my decision to have another tattoo done. I played around with designs for a while, and then asked Maria to draw it on tracing paper to the right size as it was to become linked to and around my first tattoo. Looking at it now, it looks like just one tattoo but it is important to me to know that there are actually two. This is another example of how our marriage was fucked up, but our friendship was still there – helping each other out, wanting the other to be happy. After the experience of having the first one done, I believe going back to the same place to have another one is one of the mentally strongest things I have ever done and I am very proud of myself for having done it. Once again however, my body takes over and just after I joke with the artist about how she can carry on if I pass out, without warning this time, I pass out. What a tough guy I am. The artist was incredibly cool about the whole thing. She let me recover, told me stories about people who have had fits which freaked her out so this was nothing and generally tried to make me feel a little less pathetic than I was feeling. It kind of worked, but not really.

The second example of this change, of this freedom was the charity tandem sky dive I completed. At work, we had Julia's House as our charity of the year. Julia's House is a hospice where terminally ill children can spend time to give their parents a break, where they can visit weekly, home support is given and the children can go there to die should they and their families want it. A few of us paid the charity a visit and it touched all of us. In my somewhat emotional life, this again brought perspective on my problems which were clearly nothing compared to what these families were going through. So various schemes were hatched about raising money for them and some people from the store abseiled down Guy's Hospital in London and some put themselves down to run the London marathon. I am still not quite sure how I ended up agreeing to do the parachute jump which was completely outside of what I was comfortable with. Maybe because it was because I was directly asked by a very passionate fundraiser, maybe it was because I had seen the place, and maybe because I was looking to do something different and prove something to myself and others. Had I not had the emotions of the last year forced onto me and forcibly extracted from me, I do not believe that I would have done what I still consider to have been such an amazing experience.

From 13,000 Feet (October 2010)

Falling
      for the charity chat-up line,
falling
      in love with wanting to help,
falling
      through a transient cloud of positivity,
drawing donations which are then
falling
      like rain into an ocean.

Falling
      without pure altruistic aims,
falling
      evokes strength and pride,
falling
      conjures dark humour in deeper conversation,
the antonym of just falling asleep,
falling
      for charity and falling for me.

Falling
      into the limitless expanse of self awareness,
falling,
      morphing, re-birthing,
falling
      first coupled with butterflies,
landing infused with the potency of eagles,
falling
      generating new cerebral pathways.

Whilst Julia's House got cash, I believe I gained far more from the experience in the long run. It gave me more self-confidence and possibly even more importantly, it gave and occasionally continues to give me something interesting to talk to people about. Growing up and through early adulthood I had usually felt as though I had nothing to say, and often still find myself in that situation, but this helped. I rarely think I have anything interesting to say, and so I say little, which leads to a perception of boredom and shyness, which isn't always the case. I am very rarely the centre of attention, always happy to be on the fringes looking in, but I sometimes dream of being the one in the middle, the one people come to, the one who makes people laugh at work or at parties...................... This extrovert character I lust over has a different set of insecurities and issues, but a different set of baggage to carry can sometimes make it feel lighter, at least at the start.

As 2010 began to draw to a close, I realised that Maria and I had settled into a new routine, a new lifestyle choice, perhaps drifted into it, perhaps with some element of conscious choice, but settled into it anyway. This routine included varying degrees of caginess, hope, resignation, loss. The mixture was at times disorientating, and yet often it was still comforting. I still had a relationship with the woman I had loved, my children were growing up in a traditional (ish) family unit and we were not arguing or at each other's throats. Whilst 2010 was a sex-free zone, we did sleep in the same bed sometimes, when she stayed at the house and so the possibility hung in the air, although I knew better than approach it, rationalise it or ever try and make it happen. Remember 'Relax into Wealth', don't force things and they will happen in their own time. So I was lying in bed next to the women I'd married doing nothing, paralysed. Except of course it was self-induced paralysis, and it took the mental strength of a monk to withstand the temptation to see what might happen sometimes. We were never highly active sexually and the perceived expectation, pressure, routine of sex had started to drive a wedge between us for many years before hand. In the end it all came down to control. Sex only happened when Maria was absolutely wanting it. Our sex drives were out of kilter, but whilst we had snippets of conversation about it, we were never open enough to overcome it. I only found out the key reason for this behaviour from Maria after we had separated, only when the pressure to have to make love was really off the agenda. I feel anger and loss about this lack of knowledge, but it was not within my power to guess, I was left somewhat in the dark. I would instigate what in my head was love making during our marriage, and would always try to understand when this was rejected, which was often.

Chapter 4

During 2010, we had told our family varying degrees of lies. We hadn't explicitly said that Maria and I had separated, because in our minds we were desperately trying to avoid that realisation ourselves. We told them about the flat Maria had partially moved into, and told them that this was for more creative space – which was true. So part truth, part not telling, held back by our doubts. We were able to pull off this trick of hiding the truth of our marriage to our children and family because we were still getting on, like friends do. Not arguing, working together but nothing else. It was friendship only. The new life whilst not what I would have chosen had become normal, and because I had begun to play around with poetic form a little my 'Sonnet 2010' tried to encapsulate what 2010 had been, what it meant and how I was feeling.

SONNET - 2010

Where once the wind blew, that force had now died,
Stale air only to breathe, a moonless sky,
Romance expelled, leaving only the why?
Our journey halted, malaise was our guide.
My eyes stinging with self pitying chide,
My heart racing so, my demise is nigh,
Without your love, sureness that I shall die,
Our love and my fears exposed open wide.
How then a barrenness of anger though?
Through 13 waxes and wanes of the moon,
Comfort that we have committed no sins,
Sleep does return, possibilities grow,
New life lyrics now, played to a new tune,
Journeys restart, life after death begins.

The reflection and introspection which was required to write Sonnet - 2010 continued, and as a result the following poem was written in January 2011

I will know me when.......... (January 2011)

When I don't have to guard or defend
When I can dance and sing with no fear
When I don't feel I have to play small and pretend
When I speak what others may not want to hear
Then it might just begin

When I fill any container into which I am poured
When I have felt self worth for a while
When I feel safe, grounded and secured
When I stop huffing and embrace life with a smile
Then it might begin to sink in

When I become a wandering poet
When I am open to new people I meet
When I know my dream and I dare to show it,
When romance and passion is a two way street
If these things come together, then I will know me

So I set off into 2011 trying to understand me and rationalise where I was in my life. My 'Relax into Wealth' philosophy was seemingly beginning to pay benefits. Life was abnormally normal. Our routines were chugging along, and as 2011 progressed it felt to me like we had a chance to be more than friends once more, to be married once more. We took a family holiday to Greece and there was a directive from Maria whilst we were packing about taking some condoms, 'just in case'. So clearly, and understandably in my head all was not lost with us, I just still felt paralysed, scared of playing the wrong card and unsure which way to move. However, the holiday saw Maria and I spend more time apart than with each other during the day, and then time together on the balcony in the evening, and as in England, this was mostly Maria talking and me listening. We were in a part of the bay which mosquitoes seemed to love, and whatever we tried to do didn't really work. As a family we would play a game in the evening which involved trying to catch all the mosquitoes we could. Mostly, whilst Maria was pottering around trying to get cream etc onto the kids for the night, Zoe and Ed would spot them and I would try and sneak up on them, slam a drinking glass over them whilst they were on the wall or ceiling and then use a postcard or coaster to seal them in the glass overnight. Most nights we would have 10 to 15 glasses on the table, and in the morning, those mosquitoes that survived the night (usually about half of them) would be released, no doubt to return later in the day and try to seek revenge for the killing of their brethren. Whilst I am not a vegetarian or animal activist, in my own little world and way I do try and avoid killing animals unnecessarily. I know this opens a massive debate about eating meat and the killing of the animals 'unnecessarily' but that is for another time. So I took the moral high ground in this believing that the survival of the fittest would actually help the mosquitoes population and the capture of 15 and the passing of 6 or so mosquitoes a night also ensured I managed to sleep at least a bit, although after a number of nights of broken sleep on top of the emotions being created by us being there, it did get to me somewhat.........

A Holiday Rant (July 2011)

'tis too bloody early
here in the Peloponnese
and I, pacing my balcony
am most certainly ill at ease.

My conclusion here though
is that genocide per se,
is something from which
I would naturally shy away.

But can these terrorists
Be beyond the good man?
As they mock and disrupt
my Greek holiday plan.

Me ducking whilst swishing my ears like a cow,
begins this comical scene to reveal.
I'm cursing whilst smacking my own sunburnt arms
And clapping my hands like a demented seal
Only to find them empty

They cause me to become sleep deprived.
Hot, bothered, miserable and itching.
Anti-insect cream my arse,
Now I'm in full flow best of British bitching.

Their sum is simply to spread misery.
Not to hate in my life I try.
They exact more power than size should allow,
So mosquitoes, just fuck off and die.

Whilst on holiday away from the noise of work and day to day
life, it hit me again that things were not right between us as a
couple and us as family. I remembered a guy I worked with
years ago. On Boxing Day morning his fiancée told him that
she wanted to split up. I thought at the time how awful and
insensitive, but the postulation was that she had enough time
away from work to be clear in her head that this is what she
wanted to do, and whilst they were both out of the work cycle,
even for just a few days, this was the time to deliver the
message. Again, even in the pressure situation of heat,
mosquitoes and a nut reaction from Zoe which required a high
speed car journey to a hospital in a town 30 minutes away
with the 13 year old daughter of the chalet owner giving us
directions, there was little animosity between Maria and
myself, but it would also be poetic licence to say we were
showing and feeling love. That we wanted to spend time
together on the balcony in the evening was a good sign, but

there was no softness or tenderness. We certainly cared for each other, but in a friendship way only. I was struggling with this in my head and I wasn't coping very well. I hid in my new found appreciation of E M Forster, and read 'A Passage to India' whilst on holiday, and I also immersed myself in the second album from Noah and the Whale on my I-Pod. I was struggling with everything at that point, feeling mixed emotions of wanting me and Maria to work, knowing deep down it wasn't and trying to see a way through it all. With the songs of The First Days of Spring implanted in the depths of my mind, I had one of my mornings on my own – We seemed to be planning for life as a disjointed separated family, but really, we couldn't see it at the time. Anyway, sat in a harbour side cafe having just had a late breakfast, I felt a sense of realism come over. Was it realism? Perhaps it was more like optimism? I have spent my life being accused of being pessimistic, and I have always come back with the argument that actually I am just being realistic. On this day I am not sure, but I like to think it was optimism for a change, something I have never been accused of possessing to any great degree. Anyway, I began to laugh at some of the 'major' issues troubling either Maria, myself or both of us, realising that these issues are nothing compared to the illness, poverty and death faced by so many. Those people have a real burden in their lives.

A Burden Such As This (July 2011)

When your only ill health
is being slightly overweight,
and your life stress is mainly
your well paid jobs deadline date,
when driving your children to groups
causes you to hate,
and an absence of love making
brings forth a depressive state,
then a burden such as this
is one I should like to carry.

When your holiday concern
is carbon emission and not cost,
and worrying about your kids
is only for experiences lost,
when buying non-organic mince
is a social line that has been crossed,
and when you anguish over poetic form
for feeling you are being too bossed,
then a burden such as this
is one I should like to carry.

When skin colour is only an issue
once you have been at the beach too long,
and tears flow from adults
when choosing the pass-the parcel song,
when your biggest shopping concern
is impatience of the checkout throng,
and too much time to think
causes inertia and belief you are wrong,
then a burden such as this
is one I should like to carry.

Perspective is relatively easy in retrospect, but the skill of
having it during the crisis is harder yet much more necessary.
For once I managed it, albeit briefly and as with 'A Holiday
Rant', just a slither of lightness and laughter was felt in my
heart.

Bizarrely, as it contradicts how I felt the holiday in general
went, not long after the holiday, Maria decided the time was
right to move fully back in to the house, and I readily agreed.
Perhaps my 'Relaxing' long term strategy was working! The
flat wasn't giving her the lifestyle she wanted, financially we
were stretched, and delusions of our relationship took grip
again. Had my Relax philosophy after 2 years of not pushing,
but waiting, hoping and dreaming going to make it work this
time? Sadly, and in retrospect with no great surprise, nothing
explicitly changed. I was still being viewed as inferior to her

friends and made to feel that way by her. It is true that I allowed those feelings to happen, but they were expressed so powerfully that I wasn't strong enough to bluster my way through it all. This time it wasn't the guy in the band with the campervan and alternative lifestyle from a couple of years ago that made her giddy, but a group of people organising a local festival and one guy in particular.

Chapter 5

As autumn and winter merged and the end of 2011 was starting to get close, even I, in my make believe theatre of happiness and relaxing could see us as a pair, on the stage, illuminated to the world, falling apart. Maria's birthday was the catalyst for change. I knew she wasn't bothered about us spending the evening together, so I suggested that she meet up with someone else if she wanted to. She tried to contact our friend Hannah but she was busy so Maria stayed in with me. The evening we had that night encapsulated everything about how we had become, predictable and done out of routine and obligation where she wasn't bothered about me being there. I had become so tied up and defeated that I had no enthusiastic conversation that night, I had lost any idea of what to say to her and critically I felt as though I didn't know her anymore. This was usually covered by her willingness to talk, but tonight this wasn't the case. I now know what, or rather who was on her mind but of course at the time I didn't. I brought up the subject of us that evening, saying how I was worried that we were too distant, and then, my world was to change forever. That it was over in her mind came through very clearly that night. December for me was spent in a haze, getting through day by day, working through the grief and loss of something that was supposed to last forever.

December brought 2 poems in quick succession. Contextualising them in the midst of what was happening around me, I am amazed at their overall positivity, never a regular strength of my writing, but one which upon reflection is either an acceptance that what was happening was the right thing to be happening, or it was my brain defending itself against the pain and in a perverted twist of human nature, was forcing me to be optimistic for the sake of my mental heath. If I am honest, I think it is a little of both and I am thankful.

'Perhaps' is the word of eternal hope (Dec 2011)

It was blown out of my heart
by the unforgiving cold wind.
Blown outwards from the mountain's edge
with a wicked and mighty laugh
echoing around the valley.

It was stolen from me.
From me, reeling from a bloodied nose,
lying helplessly,
with a foot on my throat
and a knife pressed to my jowl.

It was removed by a surgeon whilst I slept and
dreamt of silvery droplets of love falling onto
my head like the start of summer rain.
Yet *his* head was shaking
with pity and bemusement whilst he did this to me.
Wretchedness now that my idea of love has gone.
That two are destined to be one,
to be so right as to be inseparable
that one must die without the other.
No more.

Realisation came slowly,
and to a soundtrack of the screaming
of denial as my beliefs were agonisingly
peeled away from their rightful place
at the highest table in my heart.

Disbelief and pain reverberated through me
as I realise that I can't be
everything to her,
and she can't be everything to me.
Modern love just isn't like that.

Or perhaps............ it's just not yet my time.

Moving On (December 2011)

You will, one day soon, stand on the top of your rainbow.
A rainbow created by the sunshine of happiness,
penetrating through the tears of sadness and regret.
And you know that once you are there,
you will yell with all your being, 'thank you'
to the one who hurt you, but who did it with only love in their
heart.
To the one who stood behind you and
as gently as they could released the corset which
marriage had become and which had
restricted breath and movement and thought.
This act reawakened the beauty in everyday life,
and an uncrushed heart can again feel and cry
and even offer out love to them.
Inertia may have sabotaged your plans for action,
but that is OK, as we all need help sometimes.
So when you finally stand on the top of your rainbow,
remember the strength which was needed
to release you in this way.
Gratitude and relief will swirl around you in the form of Eagles,
and all the lies you have told to yourself will dissipate
upwards and outwards leaving a feeling of lightness.
Then scream that 'thank you' to the open sky
And be ready to move on

Despite the positivity of the poems, on the ground, day to day
over the 'festive' period brought many tears. Looking back I
really don't know how I coped, but we all do and have such a
great ability to do so. The kids watching a Christmas film that
we had watched together many times was too tough to be
around. The Christmas tree lights blazing out from within an
otherwise dark room pushed me too far, and knowing that all
had changed forever and simply not knowing what the future
would hold terrified me beyond any real life experience
suffered up to that point.

During this chaos called December, we again said nothing to our kids, families or mutual friends whilst perversely we talked freely and openly. However, I needed to confide in, release to and be myself with a friend. So during December Angela and I met a couple of times in the evening for a drink. I had worked with her previously and we got on well. Having left the store in November, we had stayed in touch and when meeting up she was amazingly understanding and patient as I confided things to her that I didn't to anyone else. The truly amazing thing about this was the ease at which I found myself being able and wanting to talk to her. She quickly became a friend who wanted to be in the same room as me and actively listened, empathised, supported and *never* judged me.

New Year's Eve 2011 though was really tough. It started with me going for a walk on my own after work whilst Maria sorted the kids and got ready to go out. I walked listening to Tori Amos, and finally ended up at a road bridge. The emotion of the music and the evening had already got to me and I stood on the barrier with my music on, crying my heart out. Could I jump? Of course not..................too much of a soft touch to do anything so dramatic and self-focussed. Pulling myself together I headed home and hid myself away blitzing down the guts of this poem which I would play around with over the following week or so, but again, against the perception I give out, it was a positive poem born out of previously untapped mental strength on my part.

31st December 2011

This is the beginning, this is not the end.
This *is* the beginning, this is not the end.
Early evening New Year's Eve and 2011 will
soon be fading photographs and memories,
but, this is the beginning, this is not the end.

This midnight resets all elements upon the Earth
and they will now embrace my voice over my silence.
My light will take precedence over my shadow and
with purpose and poise 2011 will be left behind.
Soon to embrace the excitement of the unknown, where
friendships will deepen and not be cling-filmed by clichés
and...................
I will become embroiled with a decadent blonde or red-head.

As the days and weeks speed up again,
and each morning doesn't take so long to come,
one day my new found heart will verify that
this was the beginning, this was not the end.

I called Angela that New Year's Eve and as it was our first non-work telephone conversations it was a bit awkward as we found our way through it. Nothing explicit was said, but we spoke generically about hopes for 2012. By this time my head was spinning from walking, writing and talking, and I was longing to start drinking. It was after this call that all my energy reserves fell out of me like the body of a hanged man falls through the trapdoor. My emotions were totally screwed and it then hit me that I was left in the house feeling like shit whilst Maria went out to party. I was beginning to hate how she could be so normal during December and I was falling apart, again I felt like the poor relation in our marriage. I was suddenly feeling very low and I wanted things to change and quickly. But as at the bridge earlier in the evening in my sensible and boring way I couldn't do anything dramatic and limelight grabbing, whether I was here to bask in the limelight or not. I didn't try and drink all the wine in the County together with all the tablets I could find, but just enough cheap red wine to keep me going through Jools Holland on the TV and then cry myself to sleep. The positivity of the last three poems were wiped out by this New Year's Eve. I fear physiological damage has been done by this night and only time will tell if it will last. I know that now I start to feel panicky at the thought of being on my own on New Year's Eve, but I hope that with time this too will pass.

Chapter 6

From the slow, turgid, painful pace of December, things moved quickly in January 2012. Whilst not really accepting the situation to any great degree, I was aware of what was happening around me and I knew I needed to get out of the house to be able to start to move on. Sleeping in the lounge of the marital home during December had been an awful experience, and I knew I needed to take action quickly. The second flat I found was the one I took. I asked Maria to look at it with me and wanted her opinion on it as I valued her experience and I had stopped thinking to such an extent that I feared I might miss something obvious. Emotions started to bubble, some of which I shared with others and some of which I subdued in the inner most sanctuary of my heart. All the obvious ones were there. Sadness, nervousness, and more surprisingly just a hint of excitement that I refused to acknowledge at the time as it felt so wrong and therefore it was denied access to my consciousness for any longer than a split second.

4 days until I have to leave (11th January 2012)

Where will it come from,
The strength I need?
I'm nearly beaten
And my fight is almost gone.
Maybe anger will summon it
Or it maybe the thought of another
Or the music of Noah and the Whale
Or despite myself
Or that there is no self
Or that no-one is ill or dying.
I don't know where,
I don't need to know how,
I just know that it will.

The day before I moved out was when I did the bulk of the packing. At no point from agreeing the flat to the day I moved out, and very few glimpses since, had Maria shown any emotion to me about it. Disturbingly to me at the time but somewhat more comical now was that as I cleared my things out of the bathroom, within 30 minutes, whilst I was in the bedroom packing those things, Maria was in the bathroom, cleaning, rearranging and getting me the hell out of that room forever. In my head I recall her laughing without care restricting her and whistling a happy tune with animated Disney birds tweeting along, sitting on her arm when she rested, and them helping her clear the dust from my now empty shelf all in an orgasm of joy and happiness. This may *just* be inaccurate, but that is the image I conjure up. Even with just the non-animated reality of what was happening in the bathroom I felt hurt by this but still didn't argue, question or complain. Apathy had so engulfed me at this point in our relationship. What is the point? Previously, I would make a single comment about something, and if it wasn't agreed with, I would in return get a monologue worthy of Alan Bennett espoused in my direction about how it was really important for her, or how I didn't understand. This inability to actually communicate freely was the death of us, highlighted beautifully by the symbolisms in the bathroom episode and I accept my part in this communication failure as well.

I received a wonderful text on the first evening in the flat from a mutual friend which made me smile under bleak circumstances. "Hope today was less awful than anticipated, thinking of you and sending good vibes! On the other hand, if you are sinking in melancholy and misery, may you get lots of great poetry out of the experience". A perfect balanced text, the memory of which I shall treasure forever. Those two days of moving in were possibly the most liberating of my life, the power of the emotion I felt surprised me and made me a little sad at how much I had lost over the years. *I was making decisions again. I was deciding where to put the sofa. I was* deciding which way round to have the bed. Of course I had some input into these sorts of decisions in the family house, but only if my suggestions agreed with Maria's view, and if they didn't we were back to the "I spend so much time in the house", "it is my living and work space" impassioned arguments to which I didn't really have a comeback, so she got her way. I could see that it was a valid point, to a point, so again with the backbone of a dead jelly fish, it just became easier to offer nothing. This came across as not caring, which then added to the death cycle into which we were inextricably strapped.

In early January, I started to smoke again. Never a heavy smoker, and varying from a 'social' smoker to more of a 'private' smoker by this point. My most memorable smoke at this time was in the porch of my flat in January, in the absolute unmistakable silence that accompanies snow. Watching it fall against a street light backdrop and build up on the floor was everything that one thinks it should be, and I would love to be able to write poetry about such an experience, but it often comes out as clichéd and weak. However, there were other times when I smoked in my porch where I wasn't quite so at one with myself, my situation, or the world. I was often tired or had been drinking and so the anger that I was feeling would smother my mind and feel all-consuming out there.

Social Observations on Smokers in Early 21st Century Britain (March 2012)

For the hard core smoker, the law has now
Made it tough, but they still do it somehow.
It often means only taking a draw
To this habit they have become a whore.
In all British weather they are stood there
Saying I know the risks and I don't care.
There is weird admiration of the will,
Not of those who stop, but those who go on still.

A second form of smoker can be found
The sociable one who smokes when around
Their friends who will do exactly the same
When weekend drinking or after the game.

Then there are those who smoke occasionally
When no-one is watching, so, privately.
On a rest when cycling through the forest
A deceitful smoker, far from honest
When on a ramble, going through a gat,
Or star gazing outside their rented flat.

Yes...............Outside their rented flat......................and why is
he outside that flat on his own? Well maybe it is because he is
not spiritual or "arty" enough, or he doesn't have long hair or
play in a band or organise fucking festivals. Maybe it is
because he doesn't drink that Yogi tea with those oh so deep
and meaningful little quotes that just sooooo make you think.
Or maybe because he likes watching old panel shows on
Dave once in a while rather than finding the next thing to over
analyse and worry about, or because he enjoys the silence in
a relationship and can actually be CONTENT

Many smokers say that they want to quit
If they really do, they will achieve it
Like that sad man outside his rented flat
Re-building his life, getting on with it
But as is obvious, I'm <u>not</u> that bloke,
But when's the next break? I don't half need a smoke

During January Angela and I had developed our friendship into something more. It was tentative, nervous, but real and intense and bloody wonderful. It may seem too early to have done this, but on reflection, Maria and I had been living a lie, with the best of intentions, for the previous two years, so it wasn't actually that soon after our marriage had ended. It had really been two years which is far more socially acceptable. An odd evening occurred at the marital house at the end of January during a catch up evening between Maria and myself when Maria and I admitted to each other that we were seeing other people. I started this conversation as I had done with the conversation on her birthday which led to the final split, and so I had made it easier for her to tell me about her new man. Damn! Why did I make it so easy for her??? I knew she was seeing someone and I had guessed who, but couldn't be sure until we told each other. Once again, in a natural reaction for me, I was fighting against the reality of the situation. I really do fight change sometimes.

But by the end of January, I knew totally and completely just how strong yet compassionate, loving and non-judgemental Angela was. Of course I could not be sure where our friendship and relationship would go, but I knew that at moment in time, Angela was exactly the person I wanted and actually, for reasons of her own I was what she needed at this time as well, and the feeling of being needed and wanted again brought me into the kind of state of euphoria where you end up smiling when on your own for no reason except you are thinking of someone.

As is the way, life was far from straightforward. Whilst Maria and I had been in the right sort of place to admit to each other that we were seeing each other, Angela's ex (of almost a year) took it badly when Angela told him before he found out from other people as they were still working at the same store. Tantrums came and he moved store and later left the company, which was the best for everyone. It is funny though, as I could see it from his point of view as well. I was worrying about the impact on my kids of another man being in their life and the inherent risk of me being side lined, and so I could empathise with him from that concern and it is a concern that may never dissipate, we just dealt with things differently. His reaction was to assume and accuse Angela and I of being together for years and therefore that is why they split. The tears and drama of all of this was in a very selfish way helpful for Angela and I to understand each other and it took my focus off me for a while. As I said, he and I reacted to the same emotions in very different ways. My reaction to concerns towards my children and to the new situation I found myself in was to email Maria's new man, which was perhaps an odd thing to do and Angela certainly thought I was totally crazy when I had told her what I had done, but it didn't seem to cause any additional pain or damage and it was cathartic for me.

"Well this is weird emailing you, given our set of circumstances, but releasing some thoughts to you is a feeling I have been repressing, and after a period of reflection it still there so I have decided to act upon it. Please take this email in the spirit it is intended, and there is no expectation of a reply. It is probably important to contextualise this by saying that this is written by me with a clear, logical and sober brain, unfortunately not always the case. Whilst this may not yet be an offer of a hand of 'friendship', it is an offer of a friendly hand of 'realism' and whilst I don't explicitly know that you care what I think about you and my situation, I have a hunch that you would at least be interested to hear it directly from me. Please remember that my perception is my reality. It is all I have to go on and draw my emotions from. So firstly, I don't blame you

for my marriage ending, and I don't 'hate/resent' you as an individual. Sometimes I feel it would be easier to do both of these things, but I don't.
However, there are elements of your lifestyle, ways of thinking, being, priorities etc that I wish I could take on and be like, again not just from you, but others Maria and I know. So, my point is that whilst I don't dislike you, I am somewhat jealous of your way of being (perception) and therefore reflect insecurities and doubt back onto me. This means I will be automatically cautious around you should/when our paths cross in real life............don't take it personally. I am still uncomfortable with the thought of Maria with someone other than me (again not you as a person, could be anyone) and that person being in 'our' house with her, despite me being in the early stages of a new relationship myself (hypocritical I know but allow me some human flaws). So I am not yet ready to be in the same place as the two of you, as I said to Maria, maybe around 2015? Then there are my kids and that brings a whole different level of fear and insecurities. But I trust Maria, and that because Maria and I are still working together and not against each other, especially regarding our kids, that there will be nothing to fear from you. So I'm not sure what this email has achieved, but I feel better for writing it and as I said earlier, please take it in the spirit it was intended.

I struggle to fully explain why I sent it except that it was simply part of a process of releasing and accepting the situation. His reply will remain between only him and me, but it was short, empathetic and polite and if he felt differently to what he wrote, then I shall probably never know or need to know.

Chapter 7

Much to my disbelief and somewhat disappointment, the world continued to carry on as normal, despite the obliteration of all my routines, habits, comforts and life as I knew it. My 38th birthday in February 2012 came and went and I enjoyed a wonderful day with Angela which encapsulated a relaxed and care free moment. However the emotions and experiences linked to Maria and that part of my life during the first few months of the year could be described as 'bad' or 'hard', but they were so much more than that, they were character defining, life changing, and hopefully life enhancing in the long run. They were sometimes triggered by a specific incident, word or look and sometimes for no reason at all. I did ask Angela to run away with me at one point during Easter, leaving the kids and mad ex's behind, but she declined. It was this series of texts that caused Angela to be most worried about me and my mental health, and so she did decline, but very very gently. I like to think that I would have gone if she had said yes, but I doubt it. Through the bad times there were periods of reflection, and in an attempt to be comical, the following life lessons were captured.

Key Lessons in Life (April 2012)

Love doesn't come
from anyoldpornsite.com,
and it doesn't come back
by secretly wearing the wedding ring
from a marriage long gone.

Riches don't come
from desperately playing the lottery.
You can't buy friendship,
it is that from within
which others like and see.

You don't find God
by just listening to Amazing Grace,
you have to be ready,
maybe scared, maybe lonely,
but ready to embrace.

No, love doesn't come
from anyoldpornsite.com,
and it doesn't come back
by secretly wearing the wedding ring
from a marriage long gone.

Angela was a real friend during the first few months of the
year. Happy to listen to me waffle on about my issues as they
developed and to help me contextualise my fears, whilst also
being a person I could have fun with. She was strong enough
to be able to do all this whilst at the same time we were
growing as a couple. A lesser person would not have wanted
to hear about Maria and what was going on in my brain, but
we said right from the start that we needed to be honest with
each other. This wave of gratitude, emotion and disbelief that
someone would do this for me brought a venture into a short
Angela appreciation poem. It reads more like the inside of a
greetings card than a serious love poem, but it reflects how I
was feeling.

For You (May 2012)

Yours is the credit for my smiling eyes

You are the maker of my laughter lines

An inspiration through adversity

My reason to keep believing in me

Through the complexities of life you weave

You are my oxygen, you let me breathe

I have the dominant character trait of being a reflector of things, one who needs a period of time to pass to be able to understand and accept things fully. So I spent a lot of time thinking about things and whilst I was writing new poetry, I looked back on my older writing as well. Whilst doing this I re-read the following poem. I used to have nightmares, and perhaps I will have again in the future, but it struck me that since the original explosion of the 'guy in the band with the campervan' I have had 'bad' dreams, usually involving some combination of Maria, her new man and my kids, but I haven't had my regular nightmare in which a scene is developing which scares me so much that I scream in my dream I wake up trying to scream. I don't know how to rationalise it or what it implies or signifies, but it is a fact that I haven't had a dream like this since we split up.

Leaving Dreaming Screaming (re-written– November 2010)

Foreboding morphed into fear,
in the garden of my childhood.
A smothering sense of closeness enveloped,
like a pillow on the face of a dying mother.
From grasping within a troubled dream,
within my dream state mind I scream,
like a black and white heroine scream,
when a murder in a movie is seen scream,
no holding back, raw energy, power,
stylish, with meaning,
a release of emotion,
a seminal moment.

Then

When gently oscillating between,
reality and confusion,
a pathetic murmuring whimper of reality,
heralds awareness of my within dream scream,
and it haunts me this articulation dysfunction,
for in my life I know what this means.

Perhaps I am freer to speak now? I do speak more freely with Angela. I was also at the stage of realising that I couldn't seem to write a poem, with one or two exceptions, unless it was about Maria or my melancholy when I thought about things too much. So on the way home from seeing a band one night I was set a challenge by a friend to write a positive poem. I don't think it was quite what she envisaged, but there is positivity in there. Both Angela and I have had our dreams of love broken by those closest to us and I tried to reflect that in this poem. The now anachronistic defensive walls built by both of us with the help of others from our past were starting to break up and mostly fall.

Exorcism of the Ex's (June 2012)

Anger rose
Because our beliefs turned out
To be pliable
And our pasts have shaped
This present,
Because the words "I love you"
Spat back
And became meaningless when said.

But now,
Do *we* need those words
You and I
When we have the actions?
Do *we*
Want those words
You and I
Back in our lives?
Do *we* want
To dismantle our walls of fear
You and I
And let these words flow freely?

Exorcism of the ex's
Through a mystical haze of release
With trust and truth
And patience and acceptance will allow
These words to be
Meant and used again if *we* choose it.

Ah the abundant
Beauty of choice returns into our lives.
Let's celebrate!

Having written this poem, the weirdest thing for me was that I wanted to share it with Angela, and critically I knew it wouldn't be put onto a pile of other paperwork and become a burden, something to be read out of obligation which would be procrastinated over. I was banging on about this type of emotion a lot to Angela at this point, to a point where I was even beginning to bore myself, but the novelty of being able to talk to someone about anything was still blowing my mind. But even more than that, the excitement I felt caused my heart to noticeably speed up, and there was a physical reaction in the form of goose bumps on me when spoke about intensely personal things. This was a mental and physical reaction to just talking, listening and sharing experiences with someone. It was soon after I shared this poem with Angela that we realised we did want the word 'love' back in our lives and we started, very gently and slowly, to share the words and thus our feelings, but only when the emotion was too powerful to hold back. We are very careful not to over use it for fear of it becoming devalued again so no obligatory "love you".................. "love you too" at the end of every phone call which is a relief.

That I was allowing myself to do new things and not feel paralysed was again shown in the trip I took with others to climb Ben Nevis in July 2012. The physical side of the trip was one thing, and whilst I was a little nervous about this, I always felt I could do it yet it still gives me a sense of pride that I did successfully climb it. However the real personal growth for me came in three different aspects of the trip. One was sharing the driving of the mini-bus (16 of us went) with one other guy, which meant a lot of extra pressure which is fine except I crashed a mini-bus under a low bridge many years ago which has played on my mind since then and made me nervous about driving vans ever since. The second was the risk of tiredness which often follows me around scaring me not to do too much and to go to bed early. The third was sharing a dorm with some of the other guys. I have never felt comfortable doing things like that, and as insignificant as it may seem, it broke down some barriers in my head. I have tried writing poetry about the climb, inspired by my memories and the photos, but in the same way as with the falling snow, I can never make the poems work without sounding clichéd – One day maybe.

Chapter 8

I don't live in extremes, I'm always in the middle, seeing both sides of things (hence the ying / yang tattoo). So at no point during 2012 was I at one extreme or the other on the 'depressed – ecstatic' spectrum for any length of time at all. However as summer turned into autumn and on into the start of winter, I saw the balance swing away further from the negatives towards the positives more. Angela came out with me and my kids in this time as well, and thankfully they got on well. We all went to outdoor, non-threatening places such as a music festival and later a fireworks display. Angela started to stay over once or twice when my kids were with me, and whilst it was nerve racking in the lead up to it, once it actually happened it all seemed very natural and comfortable. However issues came up which can be encapsulated by the phrase 'just life'. Things like Maria, kids, storage space, car boot sales, priorities and so on and they needed to be worked through, which I mostly did in a calm manner, but not always. It was very interesting for me to realise that I felt more anger and less forgiveness to Maria in some aspects, the biggest of which is her timekeeping – she is always late and generally doesn't care enough about that to actually make an effort to change - and it was really getting to me at this point. I thought people were supposed to be angry at the start and became more forgiving as time went on, but this was not the case for me. I seemed to be doing the reverse. I also had a throat infection around this time which laid me low for quite a while and brought back my fears about tiredness.

Tiredness kills, take a break (August 2012)

Tiredness kills, take a break.
That's not so easy to do
When you are trying to run away.
That's not so easy to do
When striving to make your name.
When living in fear of being found out if you stop
Or overtaken should you slow down,
And then panic hits when
You can't find the break to your life
When you finally decide you need it.

Tiredness kills but not in an instant
But by the apathy to life it fosters.
Slowly destroying the ability to think,
Make decisions, believe, care.
Listen, really listen before it's too late
Tiredness kills, take a break.

But the positives were beginning to outweigh the negatives. I had real moments of joy through the process of allowing myself to be comfortable living on my own. There are many benefits to it for someone like me and I have now come to accept this more. There are elements of liking being in control more, the quietness, having my choice of music, radio or television on without it being sneered at or joked about or being asked for it to be turned off or down. My mind was expanding again and life's beauty was slowly being re-discovered. Lust, laughter, fun, taking risks had all come back into my life during 2012, and I was really starting to appreciate them, not be scared by them and even begin to thrive off of them.

I read about Anacreon who was a 6th Century Greek poet and whose name lives on via a form of poetry in which the subject written about is open, but must be hedonistic and decadent in tone and nature, and in terms of form, it should be seven syllables per line.

Anacreon's World (August 2012)

1: Truth:
My truth may never match yours,
Human beliefs, human flaws.
I say in truth, I dance well,
what is it my partners tell?
My looks are an axiom
Shown though my own idiom.
We leave this world all too soon,
truth! As transient as noon.

2: Beauty:
I've had man crushes before,
but woman make my heart roar.
I've a broad take on beauty,
a non-blinkered view I see.
Music it is found within,
if you're touched, you, it will win.
Beauty found in someone's eyes,
beats that of their inner thighs.

3: Freedom:
Know your place in worldly things,
you have freedom, use your wings.
Freedom's denied by your fear,
but now is our time, right here.
You're not free through gun or bomb
give the Scot's a bloodless freedom.
Not discriminatory,
every person should be free.

4: Love:
The word love can encompass
all that exists amongst us.
As sky is around the Earth,
love lives until death, from birth.
Dionysus, he loved wine
and music, both loves of mine.
But don't say "I love you" when,
it's lust on your mind again.

All these feelings, all these emotions were beginning to rise in me, beginning to be felt by me, and sometimes this was too difficult to deal with. Having slowly shut down emotionally over the years, this release, this allowance to live again was exhilarating at times. I was having fun, doing silly things you do when you are young and in love except I was doing them aged 38. The fact I never really did anything that daring or risky when young gives an even more exhilarating rush when you do it at my age.

Finally, Fun at 38 (November 2012)

The squeaky bed-loving the night before
May have already given us away
But not her parents, kids or even I
Knew that I'd really take the risk and stay

So I lay paralysed the next morning
Listening, waiting for her Dad to leave
She was pissing herself suppressing laughter
As I could only just let myself breathe

He took forever to leave that morning
I was late now trying to do the same
But a life's lesson learnt through smiles and sex
It's more fun playing a riskier game

Chapter 9

From the fun and risks of November came December, which brought anniversaries and reminders of 12 months ago which brought the risk of relapsing emotionally. There were big things such as Maria's birthday and the conversation that changed our lives that night a year ago, then smaller things such as kids Christmas parties which felt better to be at this year than the last. But, I was fine through it all, in fact I was the most excited about Christmas I can ever remember being as an adult. I was fine through the additionally complicated Christmas planning of who was seeing the kids when, through how Angela and I would actually get to spend some time together, through the work Christmas lunch which was a particular low point last year and through putting up my tiny Christmas tree in my flat rather than the grand tree and decorations we had at the house. It was only really New Year's Eve that concerned me during December, but I had arranged to spend it with Angela and her family and so as long as that didn't fall through, all would be fine. And it was. I had a wonderful New Year's Eve joining in with a family who enjoyed simple pleasures of chatting, drinking and playing cards, who were friendly and loving to each other, and who had welcomed me to join them.

Whilst this New Year's Eve was beautifully simple, I have always had a distrust of each New Year and the imposition and expectations they bring. I have always felt that if I want to change something in my life, I would do it, whether in May, June or October. The enforced change from the 1st of January and usual failure of that change has always grated with me in the same way that no-one should wait until Valentine's Day to buy flowers or declare love. Do it when you feel it, don't just wait for the prescribed socially dictatorial calendar date. Nothing changes on February 14th, and nothing changes from 31st December to the 1st January. Change is a slow build up over time, not overnight. That said both Valentine's Day and New Year could be the prompt some need, I just hate the fact that this is so.

31st December 2012

You don't go to sleep one night a young child
and wake up hairy, hormonal and wild.
We all evolve and change happens slowly
and under the radar, somewhat slyly.
So now another ring of life has grown,
twelve months worth of experience is sown
into me, not in isolation though
but added to my prevailing life flow.

The end of the year is so arbitrary
it flouts the composite fluidity
of energy, emotion and learning
whispering all truths and leaving nothing.
From hour to hour, one day then more
and onwards on the never breaking, raw
and exposed journey of life, love and fear
continuing *through* the end of each year.

New Year's Eve gives us a chance to reflect,
or this imposition we can reject.

So as 2012 merged with 2013, I didn't set any New Year's resolutions as I walked along the beach on New Year's Day with Angela and her family seeing hundreds of other people doing the same thing. I simply hope 2013 will bring more positive adventures. I observed and absorbed the beautiful weather on that New Year's Day in a way someone can only do when fully relaxed with themselves and life. I took the brilliant sunshine to be a positive portent for the year ahead, and the strong winds reminded me of another Chinese proverb I heard once. I reflected that having survived and ultimately thrived through the last three years, how I am now better at building windmills than I have ever been before.

"When the winds of change come, some will build walls whilst others will build windmills".

Chinese Proverb